Reflections

A

WARDROBE

OF

LIFE

LESSONS

With all good blessings!
Linda

Linda Styles Berkery

Reflections: A Wardrobe of Life Lessons
Copyright © 2019 by Linda Styles Berkery

All rights reserved. No part of this book may be used or reproduced in any form, electronic or mechanical, including photocopying, recording, or scanning into any information storage and retrieval system, without written permission from the author except in the case of brief quotation embodied in critical articles and reviews.

Book design by The Troy Book Makers
Author photo by Carol Styles Hirata

Printed in the United States of America

The Troy Book Makers • Troy, New York • thetroybookmakers.com

To order additional copies of this title, contact your favorite local bookstore or visit www.shoptbmbooks.com

ISBN: 978-1-61468-489-3

MORE ENDORSEMENTS
for *Reflections: A Wardrobe of Life Lessons*

"Unique…beautifully written making it so easy for readers to identify with the understanding that the wardrobe Berkery writes of is collectively so much more than fabric, thread, and buttons."

—From the Foreword by Marilyn Walton, author of *Rhapsody in Junk: A Daughter's Return to Germany to Finish Her Father's Story*

"I still get goose bumps, when I think of the first email Linda wrote to me, and I get the same feeling when I read these essays. Linda has that something that all writers strive for: passion, creativity, playfulness, and the ability to capture the reader, whether it is in essays or in emails to a journalist living on the other side of the ocean. From Linda's heart to all of yours. Enjoy!"

—Mathilde Jespersen, journalist at the Danish School of Media and Journalism

"Linda moves between her wardrobe of dresses to a treasure chest of cherished memories with lyrical grace. She finds within the mundane a sense of both beauty and the profound…readers will be grateful they picked up this little gem of a book."

—Michael Welch, The Arts Center of the Capital Region, Troy, NY

"A beautiful memoir with lessons revealed throughout the decades. Cleverly crafted through the lens of personal history."

—**Crystal Sewell Megaridis, author, personal historian and owner, Uniquely YourStory**

"I could not stop reading. These stories took my breath away. Berkery juxtaposes a handful of poignant life lessons along a lifetime of memorable dresses. What emerges is an astonishing tapestry of a life well lived."

—**Cindy LaFavre Yorks, fashion writer, former assistant editor at *Los Angeles Times,* author of *The Side Door: Welcoming God's Divine Detours***

"In this evocative, warm, intimate memoir, Linda has crafted endearing stories that literally grow out of the fabric of her wardrobe—and her life. This is a volume to be kept on the nightstand, stories to read and re-read in the many seasons and moments of our lives. It is a true delight for the heart and mind."

—**Fran Rossi Szpylczyn, writer, social media consultant for *Clear Faith Publishing,* host of the blog, *There Will Be Bread: The Intersection of Faith and Life***

*In memory of my parents,
Jane and Bill Styles*

* * *

For Jack

*My love and best friend
for fifty-five years*

Clear now it is and plain, that neither things to come, nor things past, are...but perchance it might be properly said, there be three times: a present time of past things; a present time of present things; and a present time of future things...The present time of past things is our memory; the present time of present things is our sight; the present time of future things our expectation.

St. Augustine of Hippo, Confessions
Volume 2, xi, xx

CONTENTS

FOREWORD *by Marilyn Walton* xiii

INTRODUCTION 1

BROWN PLAID AND WHITE LACE 3
Judgment and Letting Go

A LITTLE BLACK DRESS 11
Learning Compassion

RED MINI AND STAINED GLASS 17
Individuals and Unity

SUNNY YELLOW 27
Hope and More Hope

WEAR BRIGHT COLORS 35
Service and Dreams

JOY IN HOT PINK 45
Rejoicing in Difficulty

NAVY MATERNITY 51
Loss and Life

FROM VELVET TO VELOUR 59
Gratitude, No Complaints

TURQUOISE PAISLEY 65
Strength from Fear

IVORY SILK 73
Stretching in Hard Times

MEMORY GOWN 81
Naming Mistakes

PINK DAWN TO MIDNIGHT BLUE 85
Faithful Love

RUSSELL SAGE GREEN AND COBALT BLUE 89
Aging with Grace

DRESSING FOR A REUNION 97
Unexpected Blessings

Note to Readers 109

Acknowledgments 111

FOREWORD

A single dress hanging in a closet—utilitarian, but so much more when paired with a life-changing event. Together, dresses are silent witnesses to our life's journey. Colors, prints, and textures weave a tapestry of emotions that richly illustrates who we are.

Is it any wonder that we have our favorite dresses? Reluctant to part with them, we slip them back on their hangers where they provide a reliable and tangible security that speaks to us like the soothing words of an old friend. There is an unspoken attachment that allows them to remain in our closets and our lives. The dresses might be torn or wrinkled, but no matter. Our eyes don't see those flaws. The treasured dresses have known the spit-up of our babies, the beauty of our most precious jewelry, and most poignant of all, the salty tears of our family and friends.

Reminders of past joys and sorrows, these dresses have gotten us through memorable days. Their varied fabrics have provided the familiar comfort we so desperately needed in times of sorrow and the bright, happy, colors that added to our celebratory mood in cheerful times. They showed the world our fashion flare as they saw us through milestones and the ongoing seasons of our lives. Births, deaths, graduations, anniversaries, birthdays, holidays, weddings—our dresses were there with us.

In this book, Linda Styles Berkery reflects back on her collection of dresses that helped her learn life lessons. Her essays are unique and beautifully written, making it so easy for readers to identify with the understanding that the wardrobe she writes of is collectively so much more than fabric, thread, and buttons. Linda's words resonate and endure and make us all wish we had kept the dresses that marked the chapters of our own lives.

Marilyn Walton

Author of *Rhapsody in Junk: A Daughter's Return to Germany to Finish Her Father's Story*

INTRODUCTION

*The hardest years in life are
those between ten and seventy.*

—Helen Hayes

At ten, I wasn't the moody middle child wanting to *be* noticed, as much as the one who always seemed *to* notice. I was the sorter of stories, the keeper of traditions. Reaching up or out or down, I saw invisible threads that joined people together. I still do. Now, at seventy, I'm connecting more strands. And dresses are coaching my memory.

* * * * *

Three hard white suitcases live under my bed. I yank out the middle one and plop it on the blue star quilt. I'm not loading it up for a trip; it's already full. I know what's inside: dresses, scraps of fabric from dresses, and old photos. Clicking on the double locks feels like opening a black box of flight recordings. Messages vibrate from crinkles and creases, stains and frills. Memories rise from cotton, velvet, and silk—fibers from my journey through life.

Wisdom remains on the fold of one dress. I smooth a wrinkle and kindness appears. When I trace my pinky over white lace, I remember letting go. Hope is in there too, along with judgment, loss, compassion, forgiveness…a wardrobe of memories just waiting to be unpacked. Ralph Waldo Emerson said, "Life is a succession of lessons which must be lived to be understood." I agree. But sometimes a life lesson can also be worn as a dress.

BROWN PLAID
AND WHITE LACE

Judgment and Letting Go

It was time to let go of more than just my wedding dress.

I don't usually wear hot pink. But, a burst of color can shatter my rainy-day mood. Hovering over the computer in my bubblegum T-shirt, I searched online for a dress to wear to my 50th high school reunion. Memories of those weary Catholic uniforms (plaid pleated skirts, white blouses under gray blazers) almost disappeared as I browsed through Macy's fall collection.

Playing dress-up as an adult is easy with online shopping, but not as much fun. I found a dress with three colors—blue with bands of black and white. *Perfect for a reunion,* I thought. *This will be a past-present-future dress.* One click away from completing the order, a strong thought boomed in with the thunder. *A new dress makes me feel great, but a dress can also be judged. When was the first time that happened? Ah, yes, when I wore brown plaid in August.*

---- PART ONE ----

It was going to be my first time at a country club. Although I was often fearful of my stern Aunt Marion, I was excited to have lunch with my older cousin, Katie, whom I adored. Sometimes, Aunt Marion smiled. I was counting on that possibility.

I understood as an almost-fourth-grader that a country club was an elegant place and I needed to look nice. Fortunately, I had a new back-to-school dress to wear, which was quite unusual since I wore uniforms and my family had limited resources. My mother took me shopping a few days before the luncheon. Selecting a brown plaid dress with a big sash, white collar, and lots of buttons down the front, I already felt fancy.

It wasn't often that I got to do something special without my two sisters. Being the middle girl always meant company and hand-me-downs. But this invitation was just for me. I was thrilled to be going to Aunt Marion's club without my sisters. Wearing my brand new dress, I tied a ribbon on my ponytail and paced at the bay window wishing for eleven o'clock to arrive.

Aunt Marion's shiny black Cadillac announced her arrival. I kissed Mom goodbye and climbed into the back seat next to my cousin Katie. We popped down the locks, but the car didn't move. Instead, Aunt Marion turned her black-bunned head around and stared at me. It was a long moment before she spoke.

"Why are you wearing a long-sleeved brown dress? It's *still* summer. Don't you have a light-colored sundress or something else you could wear?"

I didn't. This was the only dress that fit and I thought it was perfect.

Aunt Marion's harsh criticism withered me. I can't recall what goodies were served for lunch that day. I remember slumping down in the chair fearing that all the other rich ladies would know I wasn't wearing a proper dress for an August lunch at the Troy Country Club. I never again wore brown.

Aunt Marion's judgment of my dress expanded my already unfavorable judgment of her. I continued to fear my father's only sister. Yet, years later, I discovered a kindhearted image of Aunt Marion. The brown plaid dress story was replaced by the memory of a tiny white dress.

—— PART TWO ——

The scissors were raised. I was about to snip when my daughter said, "Wait, we need a photo. You're cutting your wedding dress on your 45th anniversary. We need to record that."

We had just returned home from bridal shopping. My daughter was getting married in the spring and I was cutting a few daisies from the bodice of my dress to trim her veil. However, a new plan took shape as I raised those scissors. I would donate the rest of my wedding gown. The material would create tiny angel dresses—burial gowns for infants who died at our local hospital. I decided to give my dress in memory of my little angel sister, Christine.

* * * * *

My youngest sister, Christine, was born on January 11, 1952. I remember her sweet smile and that she was always wearing white dresses—hand-knit by grandmothers or cotton ones with crocheted lace collars. I had a doll about her size and tried to put doll dresses on Christine, and Christine's white dresses on my doll.

I knew that Christine was a sick baby but I didn't understand why. My mother's blood was Rh negative—meaning Mom's blood lacked a protein found on the surface of red blood cells. In fact, Mom's blood produced antibodies against the protein in her children's blood. It wasn't until 1968 that treatment was developed to eliminate these problems. Until then, Rh negative blood was a big problem for moms with Rh positive babies.

A blood exchange transfusion was done immediately when Christine was born to replace the destroyed red blood cells, but Christine slipped into a coma for a brief time. My parents knew there would be difficult days ahead. And there were. Even by her first birthday, Christine could not roll over, sit without help, or stand without being supported. It seemed that her eyesight and hearing were affected too.

Years later, my mother typed out some of her memories and I read about Aunt Marion's love during Christine's troubles. Aunt Marion spent months driving my mother on rounds of specialists to seek help. None of the doctors could determine the extent of Christine's problems, and because there was no medical insurance at that time, bills were piling up. Doctors suggested that my parents put Christine in a special home, but Aunt Marion encouraged my mother to keep her with us.

Christine died two weeks after her first birthday. She was buried the next day in her tiny white dress. My parents wanted my only memory of Christine to be the sweet baby sister who looked like me. And that *is* my memory. I recall dressing her up and watching her smile. I don't recall her sickness or her death.

* * * * *

My wedding gown was cut into pieces and packaged for delivery. It was time to let go of more than just my wedding dress. I brought the white lace material to the local volunteers for *Little Angel Gowns*, and made a choice to let go of my harsh recollections of Aunt Marion.

When I think of my baby sister, Christine, I now add new images of my aunt. I see Aunt Marion with her black-bunned hairdo driving my mother around the streets of Albany. I watch her pull out her purse to pay for the extra medical visits. And I hear Aunt Marion's voice. *I'm happy to help.*

A LITTLE BLACK DRESS

Learning Compassion

*Death was as close as
my father's voice.*

Every woman has a little black dress for a night out, but mine is for day. It wasn't easy to find one that didn't shout *party time*. There's no plunging neckline or tight curves. It's a short-sleeved empire waist dress. No frills—I need to be a calm presence in my little black dress.

My primary task at the parish where I work is education for elementary children, yet I assist with every funeral. My husband and children are used to me saying, "I have a funeral this morning."

They no longer ask who died. They know it's probably not someone I knew. It doesn't matter. Every family has loss and everyone who follows a casket is in pain.

It snowed during the night so I layer a sweater over my black dress and head to work. When I arrive at church, the organist greets me with smoke on his breath. Funerals begin at 10:00 a.m. or whenever the hearse arrives. They are late today. Everyone is waiting for the deceased to arrive.

Two funeral directors lift the casket and move it inside the church next to the baptismal font. Family members arrange themselves for a procession, but there is a long line and some of them are still outside in the cold. I open another door and motion for them to come in. It's hard enough to wait behind a casket without standing in the snow. I nod in respect and smile. It never hurts to smile, even at a funeral. Tears need a gentle friend.

I greet families in my black dress at the door of our church, attentive to their needs, respectful of their loss. Most funeral directors leave during the liturgy, so I stand in the back and pay attention. I notice who might need a drink of water or a tissue.

I give a book to a crying child. I notice because of familiarity. At every funeral I remember my father.

* * * * *

Our family moved to a funeral home when I was five. I remember the first time Dad brought me downstairs. Dad whistled softly in the candlelit room, eyes twinkling as he tilted flower baskets over my head. He brought out a framed Jesus with wavy brown hair. "Here Lindy, turn the golden button and see what happens." The image lit up. I knelt on a soft padded bench and breathed lilies.

"Dad, do we live in a church?"

My father was home most afternoons. I remember coming in from school and hearing my father whistling. After knocking on the morgue door, I would yell out, "Who died?" Death was as close as my father's voice.

When I was ten, my father poured blacktop over the back lawn and built a wooden fence with a double swinging gate. Green paint went over the freshly cut wood and a lock was screwed into place. Now he could park his large black station wagon inside the yard. It was my job to open the gateway by sliding the lock and pushing on the double doors. A parked car in the backyard meant death. Years later, my sisters and I would recall that any boy we dated more than two weeks was invited to assist my father. They would lift the stretcher from the car and carry it to the morgue. Girls were rarely asked to move a dead body.

I got used to the idea that people died and what to do when that happened—answer the phone with great respect, walk to the bakery for apple squares and dinner rolls, set the table downstairs for a small meal for the grieving family.

I watched many black dresses enter and leave our home. I learned that death was always present, people mattered, food helped, and families needed kindness and reverence.

As children, we could play in the backyard during afternoon visiting hours, but there would be no piano practices on nights with wake services. We spoke with hushed voices except if the family was Irish. Then the songs from downstairs would overwhelm even piano tunes.

When we were teens, my sisters and I discovered that the funeral parlor was perfect for parties and sleepovers. Dad didn't mind if we used the space as long as we cleaned up before the next wake.

One evening, as I was washing dishes upstairs and covered in suds, the door opened. I was surprised by a visit from a local celebrity—the actress, Maureen Stapleton. Her father was being waked downstairs and she wanted a break. She tied on an apron and started drying teacups, chatting that she needed something "normal" to do. I've often thought about her comment. Sometimes the simple ordinary routines allowed grief to find a resting place.

My father taught me to whistle, hum, and not fear death. He showed me how to greet days with joy and see goodness in all who died. He never spoke those words, just eloquently modeled them. Living above a funeral home deepened my faith and prepared me for a role in parish ministry.

* * * * *

Today's funeral is finished and the procession continues to the cemetery, a thin place where the earth and eternal meet. After the final prayers, family members pull flowers from the wreaths to take home. I watch one young boy toss his rose to land on the casket as it is lowered to the ground. He creates a sacred moment without any prompting from adults.

I drive back to the parish where I work and take off my little black dress. As I change into a bright red jumper, I shake the funeral sadness away with the snow. It's almost Christmas.

RED MINI AND STAINED GLASS

Individuals and Unity

Our lives, like the colors on my stained-glass dress, can't help but bleed into one another.

There were three "jobs" that used my talent and energy until retirement—occupations that I listed on tax forms: elementary school teacher, mom of four, and pastoral associate at a Catholic parish. Two were *paid* positions. I remember wearing red during each of those time periods: a red blouse on Pentecost Sunday as a reminder of the Holy Spirit, a red T-shirt gluing valentines, and a red mini-dress teaching third grade. I wore a dress three inches above my knees because, in 1970, women working for the Troy City School District were not allowed to wear pants. I shudder now to think of how that red dress slid even higher when I wrote on the chalkboard.

PART ONE

A police car pulled up in front of our apartment in South Troy. The officer, my father-in-law, got out. "Are you ready?" he asked.

"I think so," my voice squeaked. "Thanks."

"Did I forget to tell you that I was on duty?" He laughed as I climbed in the front seat.

"You neglected that part."

I was grateful that my father-in-law insisted on giving me a ride, since I didn't have a driver's license, but it was strange to have a police escort for my first job interview. I hurried out of the car and ran up the stairs to the school office before anyone might notice.

Teaching jobs were plentiful in 1970—there were twelve openings in the elementary schools in Troy. I was hired on the spot. Leaning back in his brown leather chair, the superintendent asked, "What kind of kiddo do you want to teach?" I knew what he meant, even though it was an odd way to put it. There were eight neighborhood schools reflecting financial and ethnic differences in Troy.

The superintendent was generalizing by schools. I didn't care about financial status or types of kiddos. I was interested in transportation. I requested School 12 in South Troy so I could walk across the street from our apartment. He said, "Sure, why not? We have an opening in third grade."

I don't remember what I wore on the first day of teaching, but I definitely wore the red mini-dress the second week for the class photo. I still have the proof.

Since my parents lived only a few blocks away, I would occasionally walk up for a quick visit after school. My father was usually home in the afternoon. One day, I was complaining about how hard it was to teach such a diverse group of children. Dad poured a cup of coffee and sat down. "You know, it's just best to keep your focus on one child at a time. Don't see a *group* of third graders—see *individual* children, who just happen to be in your third grade."

Although he never mentioned it, I wondered if Dad's advice came from his experience as a POW in Germany during World War II. He spent two years in close quarters listening to the stories and needs of roommates from all over the country. Whatever made my father express those words, *look beyond groups,* it turned out to be great advice. The children in my third grade were quite distinct.

Debbie's father was a physics professor at the local college. My husband, Jack, was in his evening class. Debbie was reading at a sixth grade level. Faith struggled to read any words at all, but she came to school each day in a perfectly ironed dress—so proud that she had learned how to iron. Tony spoke only Italian and had beautiful cursive writing. Ryan stole ten dollars from my purse saying, "I took the money to buy paper." *Um, sure you did.* Billy was suspended after taking a swing at me one day. Judy was a whiz at math and bored with third grade. Veronica's mother left home to move in with her boyfriend. Veronica cried each morning for a month. "My father can't braid my hair." Probably not a big concern for her father, but it was for her. I brushed and braided her long brown hair.

As different neighborhood schools closed in the following years, more children were sent to School 12, and the range of abilities and needs grew larger. Our school moved to an "open classroom" approach.

Each child would move through personalized reading and math programs at their own pace. One hundred children from the traditional grades of 3rd, 4th, and 5th were combined under the leadership of four teachers to make my group, Team C.

My partners on Team C were very creative with the four classrooms assigned to us. Wooden boards placed on top of concrete blocks held one hundred green dishpans inside the closets. Each child had a labeled dishpan to hold personal school supplies. Three rooms were used for small group lessons and individual conferences. We removed desks and put down donated rugs in the fourth room to have a space for all the children to sit on the floor. We began and ended the school day as a large group, but the focus remained on the needs of the individual child.

Shortly after my father died, I left teaching (and mini-dresses). Home raising four children, I found another source for good advice. While I prepared supper, my little ones would watch *Mister Rogers' Neighborhood*. I would stop cutting carrots or washing potatoes to listen to his quiet words of wisdom—reminders to love and accept others just as they are. I felt that Mister Rogers was speaking directly to me.

When my children were in school full time, I volunteered at my parish and later became the faith formation director. I was teaching adults as often as children. Sometimes, I still got caught up in a group mentality, of which I was reminded, when I insisted on making an album for First Communion. When I asked for a family photo for the third time, one mom was quick to point out the problem. "Did you ever consider," she asked, "that I might be struggling with issues greater than taking a family photo?"

Fortunately, I had a spiritual mentor who, like my father and Mister Rogers, encouraged me to remember the dignity of each person. His words were wonderfully familiar. *Look for the beauty that chimes out of every individual.*

—— PART TWO ——

When I began working in parish ministry, I took a workshop about leadership and received two pieces of advice. The first was practical: Don't wear anything new when you are leading a prayer service or a retreat. That way you won't be fussing with an outfit, but will be comfortable and confident. Following that advice, I had just a few steady dresses for when I was in a leadership role.

The second advice was more personal: In your mind, put imaginary brackets around every situation, so that one pastoral experience doesn't bleed into another. It made sense. In ministry you constantly shift gears. I might walk down the hall after a funeral to find a mom and her newborn twins in my office, or go from a First Communion party to a hospice visit. But my preferred dress to wear for ministry looked so opposite of this counsel. It was a faux-wrap dress covered with dots like ink stains and multicolored swirls blending into overlapping shapes. Since it reminded me of the church windows, I called it my stained-glass dress.

One evening, I came right from my parish work, still wearing my stained-glass dress, to help a friend prepare for a 60th birthday party. My friend was living in an old mansion which had been converted into apartments on the upper floors and offices on the lower ones. The building had an old-fashioned elevator with a simple iron grate-type closure, not a door.

After loading the elevator with dishes and trays from the basement storage, we got in. The elevator was meant to stop at the kitchen on the first floor. It didn't. It stopped close to, but not at, the third floor. It just stopped. Guests were not due for another hour, so no one was around to hear the emergency alarm. No cell phones back then. An old black phone near the floor selection buttons connected us to a repair service. "We'll send someone."

My friend offered amusing anecdotes so I wouldn't be anxious about our predicament. Laughter calmed my stress a bit. I took a deep breath and countered with, "So, we should pray. Who's the patron saint of elevators? Otis?" But, after a while, we grew quiet. There was nothing to do but wait.

I plopped down and leaned my back on the elevator wall, my stained-glass dress puffed out around me. A light shone from the floor above through the black iron grate. I had a focal point in that light and was grateful for an iron grate rather than a closed door, but it was also frustrating. I could see where I would like to be—any solid floor at all—yet there was nothing I could do to get there. I could not rely on wishes or my original plans. *This is also like my spiritual journey. There's a distance from where I am to where God calls me to be. But a light points the way.*

"Hello, where is everyone?" a voice called out after about twenty minutes. *Thank God for early guests and unlocked front doors,* I thought. My friend yelled back from the elevator and gave the location of an emergency elevator key. A ladder was lowered. A hand reached down. As I climbed out, my dress caught on the iron grate. I tugged and it tore.

The elevator could wait for repair. My dress was beyond repair. After walking downstairs to the kitchen, I searched for something to hold my dress together for the evening. Since this would be the last time to wear my stained-glass dress, I didn't hesitate. I stapled all the swirls together and sat down to eat chocolate cake.

When I arrived home from the party, I cut a circle of fabric from the ripped dress and arranged it on my nightstand under the lamp. It's still there. When I look at those colored swirls, I remember that plans can be thwarted by the strangest things, and our lives, like the colors on my stained-glass dress, can't help but bleed into one another. When I can do nothing more by myself, I am grateful for helping hands that lift me out of a stuck position, and for a light to guide the way.

Some names in the essay have been changed.

SUNNY YELLOW

Hope and More Hope

Sundresses were just becoming popular in the Forties.

The first time I noticed "sundress-energy" was the morning after the junior prom. I was sixteen in a yellow gingham dress with a halter top. The short skirt showed off my long legs. *Expectations for summer love must be stitched right into the seams,* I thought. My new boyfriend, Jack, and I headed to Lake George in the Adirondack Mountains for a day at the beach. Lake George water is always cold, so I didn't bother to bring a bathing suit. We spread a blanket on the sand, ate our picnic lunch of peanut butter sandwiches, and promptly fell asleep. A lovely ending for a prom weekend—blistered. I returned home with sun poisoning.

Crawling from my bedroom to the bathroom, I wondered how a happy dress could bring such pain. It wasn't the dress. Lack of shade and lotion were responsible for the week of blisters, fever and vomiting. Sun poisoning was brutal. I was suspicious of sundresses for years.

Twenty-five years before my sundress disaster, my mother, Jane Coleman, also wore a sundress on the beach at Lake George. But she had a far different experience. Mom returned home giggling with anticipation. She had a case of summer love.

* * * * *

There was a lot of talk about the war in Europe in the summer of 1941, but Mom was nineteen and didn't give it much thought. After all, Europe was far away. Lake George was not. Mom had other things on her mind. She was looking for a boyfriend.

My mother and her friends got a ride to the lake for the Fourth of July weekend. Arriving at Hearthstone, a state camping ground, they put up a borrowed army tent for sleeping and a small tent to hold their clothes. Sundresses were just becoming popular in the Forties, and all the girls in her group shared clothes. Naturally, whoever woke up first grabbed the best dress. Mom, an early riser, found her bright yellow sundress and headed to the beach.

Mom was lounging on the sand when she noticed her friend, Alice, talking to a handsome young man. She believed he was with a group of South Troy guys and wanted to meet him. *Here's my chance*, she thought. *Alice will introduce me.* She flicked sand from her copper-red hair and strolled over, trying not to appear anxious.

Bill Styles, who would become my father, had taken a break from the family funeral business to spend time swimming in Lake George. He had been a lifeguard during his high school years and loved the water. But swimming was not the only thing on Dad's mind. He was lamenting to my mother's friend, Alice, "I've been at the beach all week and still haven't met a nice girl."

As Mom approached, Alice said, "Well, here's one I'm sure you'll like." Dad smiled at the redhead coming his way and a new conversation took off. They discovered some mutual friends. Mom was right about Dad coming from Troy—he lived just over the Congress Street Bridge from her hometown of Watervliet.

They had a great weekend, but Mom had to return to work as a cashier for Montgomery Ward on Monday. Dad offered to drive her to the bus station. Mom worried that since my father would be at Lake George for another week, he might meet other girls. She had an idea.

When they arrived at the bus station, Dad got out first. Mom secretly removed the belt from her yellow sundress and tucked it into the back seat of his car. *That way,* she thought, *I can always call and ask if he found my belt.*

Mom didn't have to worry. By the end of the week, Dad called. By the end of the summer, they were a steady couple. Years later, when Mom told Dad about her trick with the sundress, he smiled. "I guess we *were* meant to be together."

The sundress Mom wore in the summer of 1941 got packed away with the rest of her light clothes in September. Mom anticipated a return to Lake George the following year. But a different kind of anticipation would come with the winter winds. My mother and father were listening to the radio on December 7th as President Roosevelt announced the attack on Pearl Harbor. Knowing he would likely be drafted for the war, Dad joined the Army Air Corps and began his training as a B-17 pilot.

When she took out her yellow sundress the following summer in 1942, my mother's playfulness was gone. Flirting and strolling on the beach gave way to serious concerns. The best she could do was to send a photo taken in her backyard. Mom had to smile, though, as she read Dad's telegram reply:

SORRY NOT TO BE WITH YOU TO SHARE IN TODAY'S REJOICING BUT SEND BEST WISHES THAT WE CELBRATE OUR NEXT ANNIVERSARY TOGETHER. LOVE=BILLY.

Dad's wish would not become reality. He was in England by June of '43. It would take two more summers before he returned from the war.

As July turned to August 1943, Mom revisited Lake George for some solace in the sun. But her weekend of peace was short-lived when my father's sister, my Aunt Marion, showed up on Sunday. Marion found my mother on the beach and showed her the telegram, which had just arrived from the War Department. On July 25th, Dad was listed as missing in action (MIA) over enemy-occupied territory. Mom immediately returned home. Hope became her heartbeat.

News came a month later that Dad's plane had been shot down during a bombing mission. Her love was alive, but a prisoner of war (POW) in Germany. Mom's relief moved to action. She joined meetings for POW families and wrote to top brass for more information. She clipped newspaper articles, petitioned companies to send packages to the prisoners, and volunteered with the Red Cross. She wrote to my father every day. Anticipation of his release kept hope alive.

* * * * *

Although I spend time with my family in the Lake George area each year, I had not returned to Hearthstone Campground in over fifty years. On a hot Monday in early June, I threw on a flowered sundress and lathered myself with sun lotion—the strong kind. I take no chances at Lake George.

School was still in session so the beach was empty. Removing my sandals, I waded into the water and found entry to the past. Memories of teenage energy and young love splashed all around me. When I left the water and moved toward the evergreens, more years melted with the summer sun.

I thought of my parents, arm in arm, strolling along this same path, perhaps stealing a kiss. As I slid my hand along the stone wall, I saw Mom's hand trembling as she read the MIA telegram. Climbing to the top of the wall, I called out questions in my mind—questions I wish I had asked long ago.

Mom, how did you ever keep up prayers for Dad's return? Did the change from MIA to POW bring you any relief at all?

And Dad, what sweet hope energized your days as a prisoner of war? Did you ever have that anniversary celebration at Lake George? Did you return to this beach—to this pine grove—and remember?

But their voices were as silent as the stones. Answers would remain hidden in eternity.

WEAR BRIGHT COLORS

Service and Dreams

A housedress was something I thought I would never wear.

PART ONE

When she did her household chores in the 1950s, my grandmother wore floral cotton dresses with snaps down the front. The washable, "no shape/no snug" dresses moved with her as she rushed around the house. Sometimes, I noticed that Grandma remained in those practical floral prints all day long. She might be wearing the same dress when she rocked in her chair by the window at noon and when I came downstairs as she peeled potatoes for supper. After all, where was she going that required a good dress?

A housedress was something I thought I would never wear. To me, even the name "housedress" was funny and sad. I wore dresses when I was going *out* of the house, not staying home. Yet one morning at dawn, I threw on a cotton floral print exactly like my grandmother's. I was still wearing it at four o'clock when a friend arrived unexpectedly at my door.

* * * * *

I had a week alone with two children under two. My husband, Jack, was on a business trip to Oregon. *I'll be fine,* I thought. But the night he left, my daughter woke every hour crying. She was warm to the touch and probably had a fever. I got no sleep but had to be bright and sunny at dawn for my six-month-old nursing baby. I could barely stay awake.

I made an appointment with the pediatrician and hauled both children to Troy—an ear infection—the first of many. I called Jack and cried. "Can you please come home?"

"I wish I could," he replied. "But it's not possible."

The next night wasn't much better. I was really dragging. I thought about how much harder parenting was than teaching third graders. My daughter was recovering. I was not. Two full days without a good sleep really took a toll.

The doorbell rang around 4:00 p.m. I opened the door in my housedress—too tired to care. One of my former co-teachers from School 12 was standing on the porch carrying a pail and wearing pink rubber gloves.

"What are you doing here?" I asked.

"I heard you were having a rough week. I don't know much about babies or ear problems, so I came to clean your bathroom."

"What? I can't let you do that."

"Why not?" said Pat. "You need help, and I am really good at cleaning."

There was no stopping her. Pat cleaned the bathroom, the kitchen, and dusted while I nursed the baby. She didn't give me the gift of sleep, but her arrival made me feel loved and supported. It turned the corner on my mood. I took a shower and changed my clothes.

It's been over forty years since my smiling friend appeared at my door with her bright yellow pail and pink rubber gloves. But Pat's kindness remains with me. Whenever I visit a new mother at her own home, I secretly clean the bathroom in honor of my friend.

---- PART TWO ----

My children never knew their grandfathers, but were blessed with a lively pair of grandmothers. Jack's mom, Nanny, and my mom, Grammie, became best friends as widows when their spouses died three months apart. For forty years they traveled together like sisters and came to all family gatherings as a couple. Like them, I have lived to see my children's children.

* * * * *

On a shopping trip to the mall, my daughter and I landed at the Gap. She was looking for something to wear for her first Mother's Day. Her enthusiasm was contagious.

"You're celebrating your first Mother's Day as a grandmother, get something new."

I started exploring the racks of skirts and dresses and was convinced after I found a two-piece dress—a long white swing skirt inked with blue flowers and a matching top. I bought the "new-life" dress for the second part of mothering—*grand*mothering.

Wearing my two-piece dress, I began to think of my own grandmothers. My father's mother, Grandma Styles, lived downstairs in the back of the funeral home. She had a sturdy upholstered rocking chair with a beautiful mahogany frame. I saw her rocking every day until she died when I was twelve. I begged my stern Aunt Marion to let me have Grandma's rocking chair, and to my great surprise, she did. The chair was dragged upstairs to my tiny bedroom. If I leaned back too far, the chair hit skirts and dresses hanging from an open rod. But even in that tight space, I was thrilled to have Grandma's chair.

My family gave the rocking chair a professional makeover when I became a grandma. The chair returned varnished, restuffed, and covered with a lovely floral fabric, but it didn't lose the old familiar creak. The new version of Grandma's rocking chair has been my prayer chair, my writing chair, and my "cranky relief" chair. All I need is a cup of tea and a few rocks to feel better.

My mother's mother was called Nana. I was the second oldest of her twenty-six grandchildren. Nana was soft spoken and a creative seamstress. I recall her gentleness. I never heard her say anything unkind about anyone, and she lived a long life and had plenty of opportunities. I was married with two children before she died. I have her footstool under my rocking chair and her 1920 ivory hand mirror, which weighs a ton, on top of my dresser.

As I become "grander and grander" myself—now a grandmother of seven—I think about *future* memories. Even if I make it to ninety, my youngest grandchild will only be twenty-two at that party. *How will my grandchildren remember me?*

Will they remember that I rolled out homemade cinnamon bread and they braided the dough? Will one of them beg to take my grandmother's rocking chair to their home? How about the songs blaring from old vinyl records or the books I read to them? Will they know me as the grandmother who actually printed her own photos and made the albums?

I'm glad that I bought that dress at the Gap for my first Grandmother-Mother's Day. It's nice that it had two pieces. I've changed tops throughout the thirteen years, but I still wear the swirling skirt every summer. It's been to baby showers, anniversary parties, graduations, Sunday Mass, and out to lunch. It beats a housedress anytime.

--- PART THREE ---

My mother didn't wear housedresses, or at least I can't remember any. *The housedress must have skipped a generatio*n. What I vividly recall were her Saturday morning Hawaiian muumuus. The more ferns or orchids that grew in the garden on her dress, the more animated she became. All through my childhood, Mom listened to a live broadcast from Waikiki Beach, *Hawaii Calls*, as she wrapped pink foam rollers in her copper-red hair. The host, Webley Edwards, was a famous radio announcer who was the first to broadcast the attack on Pearl Harbor.

Maybe there was some interest in Hawaii in other South Troy homes after President Eisenhower signed papers creating our 50th state in 1959, but I think Mom's obsession was unique. There was one problem with her Hawaiian dream—she had no money for a vacation. But that didn't stop Mom from wearing bright orange muumuus to be ready.

"Don't make any plans for 1970," Mom announced. "Don't even think of doing anything big, like planning a wedding." I heard her message. Jack and I were married in 1969. Her twenty-fifth wedding anniversary had been planned for a decade—somehow she was going to get to Hawaii.

My sister, Carol, joined American Airlines as a stewardess in 1969. When my parents found out that they would receive courtesy airline passes, they were thrilled. As a former World War II pilot, my dad couldn't wait to get in the air. Mom was ready for her dream.

My parents were the first in the neighborhood to fly, so all their friends gathered for a party at the Albany Airport bringing a bottle of champagne right to the terminal gate. When they landed in Honolulu, Mom and Dad were presented with orchid leis, a fragrant garland of welcome. They explored famous beaches, clubs, shops and, of course, Pearl Harbor. Mom even met with one of the singers featured on her favorite radio show. She was delighted.

Since they were traveling on a courtesy airline pass, Dad planned a trip to Australia following the

Hawaii week, but when they arrived at the airport, the flight was full. My father was disappointed, but not Mom. She grinned at the extra time in Hawaii. However, her clothes were on board to Australia. It took four days for the suitcases to return, but this was not a problem. She bought a few more brightly colored muumuus and was all set.

Over the years, Mom made five more trips to Hawaii and celebrated her 90th birthday with a Hawaiian-themed party.

My mother was halfway to 93 when a two-week illness ended her life. On her last alert day, we touched up her red hair while she listened to Hawaiian music. As I left her hospice room, I said "Aloha" and closed her door. This was not planned. I had never said that to her before. Yet, how fitting that the last words she would hear would be the affectionate Hawaiian word for our final goodbye.

Mom had told me to be sure to wear bright colors to her funeral. And I did.

JOY IN HOT PINK

Rejoicing in Difficulty

Every year on her birthday, I wear something hot pink. And I remember.

If you want to make a bold statement, try wearing a hot pink dress with shoulder pads. My bright pink dress celebrated a joyful occasion after a long nine months. I wore it as a Confirmation sponsor for a young teen who lived with me while she was expecting a baby.

A tearful call came one spring morning that would stretch my faith. A dear friend discovered her fifteen-year-old was expecting a baby. My friend, of course, was heartbroken. Her daughter, Josie, was confused and frightened—she could not imagine living in her small town as a pregnant teen. They considered *all* options. I prayed silently and God's Spirit provided hope and assurance. "Remember," I said, "there is *still* cause for rejoicing—there is a new life here!" My words brought them peace and Josie resolved to continue with the pregnancy.

By the time Josie's body showed signs of the life within, she had moved to our home. Living with our family allowed Josie to keep her privacy as the pregnancy progressed. She fit right in and shared a room with my two daughters. It was snug, but it worked. Josie loved making Lego castles with my youngest children. My older son and college-bound daughter tutored her in math.

A community of neighbors, teachers, nurses, and friends from my parish church gave us support and prayers. But we also heard comments from family and friends that were harsh. "Don't you worry that your own children might see this as approval of a teenage pregnancy?"

Josie did not return to school in the fall. Her friends thought she had moved to help her aunt recover from surgery. In September, I introduced Josie and her boyfriend to the young priest at my parish, and he began to counsel them. Father Jim gave them a wonderful nickname, *The Life-Givers*.

A colleague gave me a letter from a young couple wishing to adopt, and a meeting was arranged at my mother's house. *The Life-Givers* found the perfect couple. "This is the right time for them to be parents," Josie whispered to me, "and they're the right parents for our child."

The Life-Givers got to know the adopting couple and legal arrangements were made. Over the next few months, regular letters and phone calls were exchanged. Although this was to be an open adoption, all agreed that the child would grow up with just one family. After the birth, there would be no contact with the birth mother or father.

Contractions began early on a Tuesday morning. Josie's boyfriend met us at the hospital, giving up the perfect attendance record he'd held since kindergarten. Labor progressed slowly. I called home with regular updates. "It's going to be a long night."

Everyone was exhausted, but relieved, when a healthy baby girl was born just before dawn. Minutes after her birth, I traced a cross on her tiny forehead and thanked God for her life and the spiritual strength of two teens.

"Please call Anne," Josie said. I went to a private room and woke Anne and her husband. "You have a beautiful daughter!" Our voices cracked as I shared the details. The adopting couple arrived at the hospital in twenty minutes. We embraced as I walked them to the recovery room.

The Life-Givers unfolded their plan. Josie placed the newborn in Anne's open arms and said, "I now make you a mother." Then the fathers shared the same ritual blessing. "You are now a father." The flash of smiles. The blessing of tears. A new family was born.

Josie was moved to a private room, and Anne was given a suite so she could remain at the hospital. Two days later, baby Joy was discharged to me, and I presented her to a radiant, but tearful, Anne. It was much harder than I expected. I tied the bow on her little pink dress and kissed her goodbye.

Josie celebrated the Sacrament of Confirmation in the Catholic Church five months after the birth. She asked me to be her sponsor. No one in the Confirmation group, besides her boyfriend, knew about the adoption. I wanted to wear something that would radiate my belief—there's *always* a reason for rejoicing—so I searched and searched until I found a most joyful dress.

I don't know what happened to my bright pink dress. Only a photo remains. I haven't seen baby Joy in over twenty years, but she lives in my heart. Every year on her birthday, I wear something hot pink. And I remember.

* Names in the essay have been changed.

NAVY MATERNITY

Loss and Life

*That's what I was doing—dressing
a wound by burying a dress.*

My first maternity outfit was a long-sleeved navy blue dress from Sears that I bought for my father's wake and funeral. I wore it again on Father's Day and then buried it under the lilac bush in my childhood backyard, watering the ground with my tears. The words from a homily echoed in my head. *Ritualize where you are now.* That's what I was doing—dressing a wound by burying a dress.

* * * * *

After years of infertility, I was finally expecting a baby. The positive test came shortly after I turned twenty-six—the same week my father was hospitalized for a severe headache. Dad, who would rarely take an aspirin, must have been in great pain to agree to be admitted. CAT scans and MRI tests were not used in 1974, so a diagnosis was difficult. *Perhaps* he was diabetic; *maybe* the headache was from blood sugar levels. Since Dad would be discharged with a nutrition plan on the Tuesday before Thanksgiving, I decided to wait until Thanksgiving Day to share the happy news.

On Monday afternoon, while I was teaching third grade, a call came to the school office from my mother. My father had suffered a stroke. "What's a stroke?" I asked the secretary when she handed me the note. I drove to the hospital finding Mom with her brother, Harry, standing in the hallway. Nothing they were saying made sense to me, so I waited to speak with the neurologist before I went in to visit Dad.

When I got to his hospital room, a lump of mashed potatoes was on his dinner tray. Dad's speech was choppy and he was angry. "They were feeding me like a baby." Assuring him that he would recover didn't seem to help. Dad was tired. I was tired. Mom was exhausted. We kissed goodbye and I drove Mom home.

It's funny the little things you remember from such a big time. Mom grabbed a box of Stouffer's Welsh Rarebit from her freezer saying, "Your father loves this on toast. I'm taking it to your house tonight. I'm not staying here alone." We ate our cheesy bread and curled up for the night.

Before dawn, the phone rang. Dad had another stroke and lapsed into a coma. I called my school and Mom and I set off for the hospital. The neurologist was already in the room when we arrived. There was no voice, no movement coming from my father—just beeps from machines. "He's in a coma and won't live through the weekend," the doctor said. My sisters came home and we practically lived in the waiting room outside intensive care for the rest of the week. For ten minutes each hour we could visit. *No change, no change, no change.* Dad was not living—not dying.

Eventually, my older sister, Janice, drove back to Boston, and my younger sister, Carol, flew home to Los Angeles. I drove to the hospital after school each day. At the same time, my husband drove to a different hospital to visit his father who had a brain tumor. Jack and I returned home around 9:00 p.m. each night and went right to bed.

"Hearing is the last sense to diminish," a young nurse told me on Christmas Day. "So go ahead and speak to your Dad even while he's in a coma." Leaning close to Dad's ear, I announced, "You're going to be a grandfather. And Chinese food is making me sick." I believed that somehow deep inside, my father was aware of the new life within me. I wanted to share the details.

We did NOT ring in the New Year of 1975. Dad was still in a coma—*no change, no change.* On January 6, 1975, forty-two days after the stroke, my father was transferred to the Albany Stratton VA Medical Center. The hospital was reluctant to accept him at first. But my mother insisted. "If you don't provide a bed for a veteran who was a POW in Germany for two years, I will call every single news station and put up a fight." They understood. Mom was caring for her airman once again.

We waited and watched for seventy-five more days. The child within me grew stronger as my father's body weakened. I continued the one-sided talks on Saturdays. "I felt the baby kick...We picked names, but don't tell Mom...The crib is set up...Grandma's rocking chair is in the nursery...My clothes are getting snug." On March 17th, St. Patrick's Day, I sang

Too-Ra-Loo-Ra-Loo-Ra, Dad's favorite Irish lullaby, the one he always whistled. Five days later, after 117 days in a coma, Dad died. It was time for a final kiss, time to buy a maternity dress.

It was Holy Week when my sister, Janice, took me to Sears. Other sisters were shopping for Easter dresses, but we headed to the maternity section. Peeking at the mirror in the dressing room, I gazed at my enlarged belly as Janice handed me a long-sleeved navy blue dress. The dress had a white collar and white cuffs. It buttoned all the way down the front and tied in the back. Easy on and easy off. "Don't you want to try anything else?" my sister asked.

"No. I'm done."

This is real, I thought. *I'm wearing a maternity dress for the first time at Dad's wake and funeral. Even growing up in a funeral home couldn't prepare me for this death.*

After Dad's burial in St. Joseph's Cemetery in Troy, I hung the dress in the back of my closet and never looked for it until June. On Father's Day, I wore the navy dress to Mass and remembered Dad in my prayers. When I returned home from church, my husband, Jack, ran out to meet me. "We need to get to the hospital. Now *my* father died. Can you believe it? He died this morning—on Father's Day."

The street outside St. Mary's Church in Troy was lined with police officers standing in the hot sun to honor one of their own. I walked in the funeral procession wearing the navy blue dress for the third and final time. Returning from the cemetery, sweaty and tired, I grabbed a white plastic bag from our car and climbed the stairs to my mother-in-law's home for lunch.

Excusing myself after eating, I locked the bathroom door and slid off the hot dress, my slip, and stockings. I grabbed a washcloth and wiped my face. After rubbing cool water over arms and legs, I opened the white bag and took out a change of clothes. I pushed my arms through a pink sleeveless top and pulled on a pair of shorts.

The moment I stepped out of that dress, I felt different. Lighter. Aware. I was carrying a new life—had been all along—but now I could finally breathe. I glanced in the mirror and saw myself as a mother-to-be. I shoved the dress in the bag and tossed it in the car. The dress was easy to remove, but not the grief. Shifting my focus to new life, I decided to take one small step.

The following week, on my final day of teaching elementary school, I drove to my childhood home only two blocks away. I pulled the navy maternity dress from the white plastic bag. My mother was at work. But I didn't need her. I knew where my father's garden tools were kept. I grabbed a shovel and began digging in the dirt near the lilac bush—Dad's favorite bush. It didn't take long to scoop a hole big enough to bury a death dress.

Six weeks later, on the first day of August, my waves of grief were overtaken by waves of contractions. The birth of a daughter put things in reverse. I carried my child on the outside, and my father within—his presence always near.

FROM VELVET TO VELOUR

Gratitude, No Complaints

*I was in love with a
blue velvet jumper.*

Long before Bobby Vinton ever sang about blue velvet in 1963, I was in love with a blue velvet jumper. It came with a white blouse with puffy sleeves covered with blue velvet polka dots. The jumper must have been expensive since it had to be dry-cleaned. I can't imagine my mother buying such a fancy dress. Maybe it came from Aunt Marion. I remember petting the velvet to watch it shimmer and shine and the proud way I twirled. I was a seven-year-old princess going to the ball.

In my late twenties, I ordered a dress made of "crushed velvet" using birthday money from my mother. I wore it to church and Christmas dinner that year, but where else could I wear a blue velvet dress? I only danced at imaginary balls with two toddlers standing on my shoes. The dress lingered at the back of my closet for years until I finally stuffed the fabric and made pillows for our couch. At least I could feel the velvet while resting my head for a nap.

Blue velvet remained my "high bar" for a magnificent winter dress, but, eventually, I settled for a blue velour bathrobe—an evening dress that was way more practical. In our early years of marriage, my husband would drape the robe over the tall radiators in the hallway to let it warm up—such a sweet thing to do. Once again I felt like royalty wearing "sort of" blue velvet.

But after years at home with children, my blue robe showed signs of age. The plush was gone. It was faded and frayed on the cuffs and neck. The pockets were full of tissues that dried tears, with pennies from the stairs, and a leaky magic marker. The hem unraveled, two buttons were missing, and bleach had stained the zipper. I wanted richness back in my life.

One year, when my children were young, my birthday fell on a Sunday. I anticipated homemade cards, sweets, and a gift—something small but wrapped with love. I imagined a simple family party and some chocolate cake. After peanut butter sandwiches, I was handed a gluey card from my two little boys, an effort organized by their eight-year-old sister. But there were no gifts to open and nothing special for dessert. This was so different. My husband usually took the children shopping or at least picked up a grocery store cake, but Jack had been taking graduate level courses at night after working all day. He simply forgot.

I pulled out a container of frost-covered vanilla ice cream and jammed a candle into it. The children sang. I pouted. *There should be cake. And a surprise. Why did I have to plan a celebration for myself?*

Self-pity took hold, and my husband noticed my tears. "I'm so sorry," he said. "I'll bring the children next door and we'll go to Macy's. You can select something nice."

Jack had never shopped with me before, but clearly he was making an effort. He was uncomfortable with my wandering. I took my time browsing through sweaters, pocketbooks, and jewelry. I wanted something special. I *needed* something special.

When I felt the velvet cranberry bathrobe, I knew I had found the right gift. Grecian braids at the collar were perfect. The pleats were generous and soft. Crystal buttons sparkled. It was expensive, but I justified the cost. *This lovely robe can replace the old blue one. I will curl up on the couch and relax in luxury.*

I cut the tags as soon as we got home and modeled it for the children. I was careful not to let anyone touch the robe to keep it birthday clean. My indignation over being forgotten was soothed. Or so I thought.

The following nights I wore the cranberry robe watching TV or reading in bed, but memories of my tears and disappointment lingered like a smudge on a window you were sure you cleaned—until the sun appeared. The soft rich fabric failed to mute the playback of a whiny voice. *You forgot to get me a gift? There are no presents to open on my birthday?*

The old robe came out more often. I didn't want to ruin the new one. But, truthfully, I felt more loving and gentle wearing "old blue." I had moved my focus from complaining to gratitude.

Both robes hung together on the back of our bedroom door for years until we moved to a new house. I didn't want to move the image of my whiny self so I tucked the cranberry robe into a pink fabric box and gave it away.

* * * * *

I still wear my blue bathrobe on winter evenings. I've learned that even if I'm wearing an old robe, I've been wrapped with love that never seems to fray. That's real royalty. But I *did* find a blue velvet scarf for when I need to touch that love and dance like a princess.

TURQUOISE PAISLEY

Strength from Fear

You can't imagine a stroke on a thirty-ninth birthday.

In October of 1988, I balanced a jug of apple cider in one hand and a homemade apple pie in the other and boarded a plane. My heart was pounding. I had never flown alone or been away from my husband and four children for more than a day. I traveled on standby status from Albany to Chicago to Dallas to Lafayette on my brother-in-law's courtesy airline pass. I was all dressed up in a turquoise paisley dress.

Family and friends thought this trip was a happy-fortieth-birthday present like the paisley dress.

But I knew better—this was a "courage" trip for me. Only a few people knew that I was heading to visit my former pastor in order to make a spiritual retreat—a time for quiet reflection after a difficult year. My husband, Jack, had fully recovered. Now it was time for me to move forward. *Forty will be great,* I tried to convince myself, *especially after the stress of thirty-nine.*

* * * * *

On a cold January day with a brilliant blue sky I was roasting a turkey and frosting a cake for my husband's 39th birthday. The baby was napping and four-year-old Tommy was upstairs with his new friend, Glenn. Lego music—clinking, dumping, swishing—blended with giggles. I remember checking the clock when the garage door opened. I wasn't expecting Jack until dinner.

"Why are you home so early?" I asked. Jack mumbled, grabbed some Tylenol, and climbed upstairs. I quickly basted the turkey and followed him to the bedroom. I had known Jack since we were fifteen. He had never complained of headaches nor left work early, and though he was always a man of few words, the mumbles were odd.

Something is terribly wrong, I thought, as I crawled under the covers with Jack. Stroking his head I prayed for understanding. I didn't feel panic or fear—just a strong awareness that this wasn't a simple headache.

Jack fell asleep and I went downstairs. I called little Glenn's mom, a nurse, and she offered to take the two children. "It's probably something ordinary—nothing to worry about," she said, hustling the boys into her old wagon.

You can't imagine a stroke on a thirty-ninth birthday.

That afternoon Nanny, Jack's mother, stopped by. I was really glad to see her since this day was rapidly changing. When Jack awoke, I became alarmed. He tried to speak but nouns and verbs were jumbled, syllables were out of order. And to add to the pressure, he was aware of his speech problems but refused an ambulance. Jack's favorite turkey dinner, along with the baby, were left in Nanny's care as I drove him to the nearest hospital.

The ER doctor guided me through the admission. "You need a cardiologist, but I am not allowed to make a recommendation," he said. "However, if you were to tell me that you heard Dr. D. was a wonderful physician, well, I would certainly agree." I was grateful for his clues and requested Dr. D. After Jack was attached to a heart monitor and admitted for observation, I drove home feeling very alone.

We thought there had been no warning for Jack's stroke until he remembered a brief comment from his childhood pediatrician. "Your heart valve might cause a problem as you age due to that case of rheumatic fever."

My husband was a runner in good physical shape. Just the previous Sunday, he had spent hours making and painting "snow helmets" with the children to celebrate the Super Bowl. We learned later that the stroke occurred when a flick of scar tissue around the aortic valve traveled to the brain. Being strong and healthy made no difference in Jack's case.

The children were sleeping and my mother-in-law was on the couch when I arrived home at midnight. After Nanny left, I started to turn off the dining room light. I had remained calm, confident, and strong throughout the driving, waiting, and testing. However, when I saw the birthday cake, children's cards, and piles of sloppily wrapped gifts on a dining room table, all waiting to be celebrated with their father, I collapsed into tears.

In less than twelve hours my plans for a celebration changed into plans for recovery and prayers for a longer life. Lighting a single candle on the chocolate cake, I prayed for thirty-nine more years of life and love.

Later as I crawled into bed, I grabbed a small book of prayers and opened to a letter written by St. Francis de Sales (1567-1622) to his dear friend:

> *Do not look forward to the changes and chances of this life in fear; rather look to them with full hope that, as they arise, God, will deliver you out of them…Do not look forward to what may happen tomorrow; the same everlasting Father who cares for you today, will take care of you tomorrow, and every day. Either He will shield you from suffering, or He will give you unfailing strength to bear it. Be at peace then, and put aside all anxious thoughts and imaginations.*

I returned to that passage each morning and practiced the advice by journaling my gratitude: "Neighbors shoveled snow… a friend brought milk… a co-worker took the children to lunch." The grace of gratitude showed. Nurses commented that I had appeared calm during all the testing and difficult decisions.

Jack and I spent the year settling back to "normal." After a few months there were no lingering physical effects from the stroke-birthday and we could begin to relax. When Jack turned forty, I felt the emotional release of what might have been.

* * * * *

As I descended the steps of the small commuter airplane at the Louisiana airport, the turquoise paisley dress felt cool against the heat and humidity of the afternoon. I spotted my former pastor and headed to the retreat, grateful for the invitation to rest, reflect, and write. I had made it halfway across the country.

The week brought a sense of calm and gratitude for life. I stopped looking back with worry and I began to look ahead with joy. *Jack and I will have many more years together.*

I never took a photo of my courage dress, but when the dress got snug, I used the fabric to make a pillow for the rocking chair next to my bed. I think about the swirls of life every morning when I use the paisley pillow as a lap-desk to write in my journal. If I seek courage or I begin to feel anxious about the "changes and chances" in life, I re-read the prayer of St. Francis de Sales, hug my dress-pillow, and take a breath of gratitude.

IVORY SILK

Stretching in Hard Times

And now my father—through his silk parachute—would be present at her wedding.

"Walk over to me," I said to my daughter, Leanne, as she modeled her wedding gown. "As you move, it's happening again." The lining was hanging below the hem of the dress even though we thought we had fixed it. The lining seemed to stretch each time my daughter moved. *What was going on?*

Leanne got engaged in December 1996 and two weeks later, my husband lost his job. We planned for her July wedding on a very tight budget. Fortunately, she wanted a simple slip-dress, a popular style that summer. My sister, Carol, made the gown and mailed it from Colorado along with a note saying the dress held a surprise. No wonder it stretched. The lining was made from my father's World War II parachute.

The future bride was the child within me when my father lingered in a coma for four months before he died. She grew as he declined. Her birth was such a joy for our grieving family. And now, my father—through his silk parachute—would be present at her wedding.

I stroked the lining of my daughter's gown and remembered one of the few stories Dad shared about his war days on a B-17—he never had time to use his parachute. After his plane crashed in the middle of the North Sea, Danish fishermen saved his life.

As a child, I pictured kindly "apostle-like" fishermen with a boat close to shore. My child's mind never quite grasped the impact of that day. *Dad was safe, but he was taken as a prisoner, so maybe the Danish fishermen weren't so great after all.* It would be years before I understood and appreciated the full story of his survival.

* * * * *

On his eighth mission out of England, July 25, 1943, Dad's aircraft was hit by intense shrapnel-filled ground fire (flak) as they flew to heavily-defended Kiel in Germany. It was too late for ten men to bail out. Heavy with bombs, the B-17 crashed into the North Sea seventy miles from Denmark and nearly triple that distance from England.

Co-Pilot Dad and Pilot Carey escaped the quickly sinking plane. Two severely injured gunners were pushed through the overhead hatch by the other six crew members. The brave "pushers" were then trapped in the radio compartment and sank with the plane. A friendly bomber circled low intending to blow the rubber dinghy toward the survivors, but instead, it blew the boat further away. Four shocked Americans floated in their life vests.

Dad must have been terrified. He didn't know that the skipper on a small fishing boat named *Bertha* saw the American plane go down. The fisherman quickly pulled back the nets and went searching for survivors. Within the hour, Dad and the three others were pulled to safety.

Language was not a barrier to kindness and courage. The Danish fishermen, Svend and Viggo, used splints from a wooden fishing crate to set broken wrists and legs. They wrapped the two injured gunners in blankets tied with fishing rope. After giving the pilots warm clothes and sharing whatever food they had, Viggo took pictures with his new camera. In one photo, Dad is leaning against the rails, struggling to smile as fear rocks him like the waves.

Pilot Richard Carey (left) and my father, Co-Pilot William Styles (right) on the Danish rescue boat, Bertha, on the North Sea, July 25, 1943

The fishermen and flyers waited six hours in case an American plane returned. When it was clear that an American rescue would not happen, Svend and Viggo expressed sympathy and explained they did not have enough fuel to reach England. Since *Bertha's* catch of Americans had been observed by a German fighter plane, the Danish fishermen were obligated to bring the flyers to the closest port. Near midnight, *Bertha* set course for Esbjerg, Denmark.

When the cutter boat arrived at port the following afternoon, the two pilots were brought to the German authorities. The injured gunners remained on the boat for several more hours. They moaned in pain despite outraged protests from local Danes who shouted for an ambulance to collect the wounded. The four surviving crew members never saw each other again.

My father handed over his only possessions: a crucifix on a chain, a cross, a pocket lighter, a watch, and ID dog tags as he entered the interrogation complex in Frankfort, Germany where he was fingerprinted and photographed. He spent nearly two years as a POW in Stalag Luft III and later in Stalag VIIA.

Dad never shared much about his time as a POW, except to express gratitude to the International Red Cross which provided extra rations, books, and a log.

He read over 250 books, drew in his journal, and held discussions with his roommates. From the list of debate topics, I recognize the constant fear. *When the Russian army advanced, would all the POWs be moved or killed?* And yet hope was present in the last recorded debate. *Is there really an inherent goodness in all mankind?*

On April 29, 1945 the overcrowded POW camp Stalag Luft VIIA was liberated by advance troops of Patton's Third Army. Dad always claimed that he was so overjoyed about his freedom that in running from the camp, he nearly knocked down the general, who apparently told him not to worry. According to Dad, Patton said, "I would be running too if I had just been released." Whether it was Patton or another general that Dad ran into, I will never know for sure.

Around the first week of June 1945, my father arrived home to Troy, New York, thirty-five pounds lighter. He and Mom were married in July. They had a backyard reception with food bought from donated ration stamps. After a short honeymoon in New York City and a two-week rest, Dad headed to Texas for advanced training.

My father wanted to remain active in the Army Air Corps as a flight instructor. However, by the end of October, Dad discovered that he wouldn't qualify as a trainer due to his lack of flight time. Since he spent two years as a POW, he did not have as many hours in the cockpit as other airmen wanting the position. Dad handled the disappointment with calm and grace. My father brought home his newly issued parachute and focused his energies on a different path. He went to embalming school on the GI Bill and officially joined the family funeral business.

* * * * *

The lining of the wedding gown, created with Dad's parachute, was hemmed to a much shorter length. My daughter was radiant in that simple dress. Twenty years after the wedding, Leanne's dress still lives in a suitcase under my bed. I keep the gown inside-out to occasionally finger the silk. I tug on the fabric and picture my Dad as a young man stretching to meet his hard times without any stain of bitterness. I am reminded to do the same.

MEMORY GOWN

Naming Mistakes

*Hospital gowns are
vulnerable dresses.*

Hospital gowns are vulnerable dresses. I've worn them giving birth, after surgeries, and in the emergency room for one peculiar episode.

One January evening around bedtime, I experienced something called transient global amnesia—a sudden loss of memory. There was no trauma to my head and no obvious cause. Perhaps the medicine I was taking for a sinus problem was too strong, but the doctors were not sure. My ability to create new memories and to recall recent events merely vanished for about two hours.

I repeated questions in a five-minute loop. "What day is it? Oh, Sunday—what did I do today?" I calmly asked my husband over and over. My memory was frozen like a needle unable to touch the record in my brain.

My cognitive thinking was clear. I followed directions. When my husband, Jack, called an ambulance thinking I might be having a stroke, I changed from my nightgown and chose the hospital by name. I could state my birthday and find my purse but I had no recall of any of those actions or conversations. Later, when Jack recounted the particulars of that evening, it was like hearing a story about someone else.

Transient global amnesia is rare and short-lived. No one really knows why it happens. When the ER tests were clear, I happily shed the hospital gown. The neurologist explained that I was highly unlikely to have another episode and offered some advice.

"Don't even try to retrieve the memories," he warned. "They are simply gone forever. You cannot get those hours back, no matter how hard you try, so don't try."

As we drove home, I pondered the amazing work of our brains—recording our thoughts and events.

Then it hit me. There *are* moments that I'd like to forget. There are arguments I hope my children forget—times when I missed the mark as a mother. Wouldn't it be nice if *those* memories were gone forever? Not faded, but gone, never to be retrieved.

Our family had a tradition when the children were young. When there was a disagreement or problem, we taught our children to say, *I'm sorry that I…* and *name* the problem. The offender then added: *Please forgive me*.

The pattern caught on quickly: *I'm sorry that I knocked over your Lego castle, please forgive me*. The words, *that I…* became routinely attached to any *I'm sorry*. However, I never realized the significance of this ritual until our children were teens.

One evening my daughter showed me a lavender dress she bought for an upcoming family event. I didn't like the dress at all. As she modeled, I criticized. "That dress looks awful on you," I said. "It makes you look so heavy in the way it clings around the waist."

When I saw her teary face, I knew I had hurt her. I didn't know why I said those awful things aloud. It wasn't like me at all.

"Oh honey," I said. "I'm sorry—really, I'm sorry."

My daughter moved closer and using rolling hand gestures she simply said, "*that I...*" and waited. She needed me to name the hurt and follow through. I choked up.

"I am so sorry *that I* made such mean comments," I said through my tears. "I'm sorry *that I* was rude. I'm sorry *that I* shouted. Please, forgive me."

Saying "I'm sorry" was not enough. Naming the hurt and asking forgiveness allowed our relationship to begin healing. I gave her a small hug. She nodded and went upstairs to put away the dress. I wondered how I could have spoken so harshly and cried myself to sleep.

A few weeks later, my daughter wore the lavender dress to the special event. I helped her zip up the back, and she smiled. She didn't seem to have any lingering hurt feelings. Perhaps this dress conversation was lost in my daughter's memory. Unfortunately, it will never be lost in mine. Maybe it's better to remember.

PINK DAWN TO MIDNIGHT BLUE

Faithful Love

The dress made the same swishing sound as I walked or waltzed with Jack.

On New Year's Eve when I was fifteen, I met a wonderful guy named Jack. We danced all night at a house party until 1964 arrived. Three weeks later he gave me his class ring and we became a steady couple.

I invited Jack to my first prom at C.C.H.S. (Catholic Central High School) the following May. I remember the excitement of choosing a formal prom dress. I found a pastel pink one that I loved, but it had spaghetti straps. Girls at our Catholic high school were required to have at least three-inch straps or sleeves. The dress was too long anyway, so I cut the hem and used the material to make very thick straps. It worked.

I loved all that went with that first formal dance—finding high heels, getting my hair done for the first time at a beauty shop, makeup put on by my older sister, photos taken on the front steps of the house, and carrying a bouquet of sweetheart roses. Jack and I danced till midnight mostly to the sound of the Beatles. I especially loved the way the dress made a swishing sound every time I moved.

After many more high school proms, college years, our wedding, raising four children, and becoming a grandmother, I started a search for what would likely be my last formal dress. Three of our children were already married, and our youngest was getting married in the spring.

I didn't want a typical "mother of the bride" outfit. I wanted an adult version of a prom dress. Seven dresses later, that's what I found—a beautiful midnight blue gown with swirls of stitching around the bottom and wide straps to cover aging arms.

Some things were familiar—silver sandals, hair and makeup done in the morning, photo sessions. The dress made the same swishing sound as I walked or waltzed with Jack.

Our daughter, Mary, began a new tradition at the wedding reception. Instead of throwing her bridal bouquet to all the single girls, she had a plan. The disc jockey called all couples to the dance floor. Little by little the dancers dwindled as he asked couples who had been together for at least five years to keep dancing and everyone else to sit down. Then he called out ten years…keep dancing…twenty…thirty…forty…fifty. Fifty years had passed since our first prom and Jack and I were still dancing.

Mary presented her bridal bouquet to the last couple remaining on the dance floor, which turned out to be us. She thanked us for our many years together. The bouquet was white tulips, not sweetheart roses. My dress was the color of midnight blue, not pink clouds at dawn. But my date was the same wonderful guy named Jack.

RUSSELL SAGE GREEN AND COBALT BLUE

Aging with Grace

Seventy, though, seems to be made more for quiet reflection than dressing up.

— PART ONE —

My only green dress was not the emerald shade I imagined I would wear in Ireland, but one that I was forced to wear entering Russell Sage College in Troy, New York. It was a tennis-type dress of sage green with cold metal snaps down the front and shorts attached under the skirt.

I never had a physical education class until I began my first year of college. St. Joseph's Elementary School and Catholic Central High School did not have a program for girls. When I was handed a package at college orientation containing a one-piece gym dress, I was concerned. And I was right to be worried. Not only would I have to take a physical education class, I was scheduled (by mistake) for the group time with all PE majors.

Walking into the gymnasium in my green gym dress, I took a glance around. Most of the equipment was completely new to me. I knew how to ride a bike and had played softball for one summer in sixth grade, but I never saw gymnastics equipment until that morning.

Fortunately, the class was large and the other girls were overly enthusiastic. I realized that they would gladly take my turn on the horse, uneven bars, balance beam, or anything that was put in our way. If the teacher wasn't looking at our section, I would simply say, "Go ahead, you can have my turn." And hiding behind those physical education majors worked.

That plan got me through the first semester. I passed with a C grade, the lowest grade of my entire academic career, but second semester was easier. I knew how to swim. I never did learn to dive, but I had no trouble swimming laps or treading water.

Now, in retirement, I am more physically active than I was in college. I will never be an athlete or do gymnastics—some things will never happen—but I've gained confidence with my aging body. Even with aches and pains, I've learned that it's never too late to exercise for health. Deep water movements help the arthritis in my knee. I make time for yoga and lifting weights. Because life is short, I don't hurry my walks. I take small steps and savor. But I do not wear a dress of any color when exercising.

PART TWO

While testing compounds for electronics in 2009, researchers at Oregon State University discovered, quite accidentally, a brand new pigment they named YInMn Blue. After a problem with chemicals in my hair, I discovered a similar shade, cobalt blue, also quite accidentally.

My body speaks to me, but I don't always pay attention. Even the hairs on my head have a voice, and they were singing like a rock band one afternoon. I heard their vibrations and felt stings as I drove home from the beauty shop. A quick glance in the mirror showed scarlet patches on my neck. I thought it would be best to rinse off the coloring product. I was wrong. The hot shower drew my entire body into hives and my throat to itching.

Antihistamines put me to sleep and the next morning an allergist gave me a warning. No more hair dye. Never again. Over the following months, I cut and cut the remaining mahogany color from my hair. I would be all gray at fifty-four.

The doctors had their own explanation for my stinging, singing hair. They thought I had too much exposure to chemicals as a child growing up in a funeral home. But I have my own idea. The day my hair played loud music was the anniversary of my father's death. He died at age fifty-four—my age. I believe my body was stressing in rhythm with Dad that sunny March afternoon.

Losing the color of your hair seems like a minor problem, but it was an adjustment. The transition took a while. After a few months, only a streak of brown remained hidden under silver-gray. I felt faded. I felt like I had lost my spark. As my brown disappeared, I searched for ways to brighten my face.

I came across the gift of cobalt blue when I tried on a dress for an anniversary party.

Cobalt blue is an easy shade to find now, but years ago, there were few dresses or tops in that color. Whenever I found one, I bought it. My children think it is the only color I wear and they are almost correct. It remains my favorite color. There is something radiant in that shade of blue. I come alive while wearing it.

Silvery hair didn't necessarily bring me wisdom. That comes when I slow my spirit and let the signs of aging unfold. Life will continue to ask me to let go of something, but life also has a way of bringing new gifts to every age and season.

—— PART THREE ——

"Well, of course you're looking at wind chimes, you're old." That was the comment from my daughter, Mary, when I told her I was browsing for something new to celebrate turning seventy. I'm not sure how wind chimes connected to aging in *her* mind, but she got me thinking. *What chimes out from me?* I hope a gentle voice comes with this new decade—that my words might ring of encouragement and love.

After I hung the wind chimes on my porch, I "Googled" the word seventy and found interesting facts. Counting from one to seventy takes about thirty-five seconds. Seventy percent is the benchmark for good chocolate. Seventy percent of all writing gets tossed. Copyrights expire at seventy. In some Asian cultures, seventy is considered the "Rare Age of the Olden Times." Atomic number 70, Ytterbium, is a silvery lustrous metal that slowly oxidizes in the air forming a protective layer. A protective layer sounds great. Maybe the days of seventy are all about honoring and preserving the experiences of life.

When I turned forty, I wore a turquoise dress. At fifty, it was a maxi floral print. At sixty, I wore a cobalt blue dress which highlighted my silver-gray hair. Seventy, though, seems to be made more for quiet reflection than dressing up. So far, arriving at seventy has felt like living in jeans and yoga pants, wearing flat shoes and always having a hat—for the sun, or for the wind. My energy comes from giving away and giving back. Dresses, books, treasures—like fancy purses and silver shoes—have been marching right out the door. I am gathering memories, not things.

Perhaps each new decade deserves a new dress, but I also want to celebrate inner renewal, the linings of me. Surviving the Sixties and my sixties has left me with plenty of stories. Like seasonal sorting of clothes, I arrange the shapes, colors, and sizes of the 25,567 days that make up seventy years and hold them in gratitude. On this milestone birthday—serenity at seventy—I will write of the strengths I've gained, the lessons learned. Writing is a good ritual for an old gal in a new dress.

DRESSING FOR A REUNION

Unexpected Blessings

I'm standing in the middle of memory and expectation.

At the Hyatt Regency Hotel near Dulles Airport, I'm wearing the same tri-colored dress that I wore for my 50th high school reunion in 2016—it's mostly blue, with bands of black and white. I call it my past-present-future dress. The dress is making an encore appearance in 2017 at a *different* reunion tonight. *Can it really be called a reunion if we've never met?* My husband tells me to hurry. We exit the elevator and enter a full dining room. The celebration begins.

Arms reach across the table to shake my hand. A shoulder nudges close. I feel a tap on my back. Legs move toward me. Fingers clasp. Another arm extends around my waist. Then hugs, so many embraces and tears. I am aware of my middle-ness. I am a quiet middle child, in the middle of a loud story. I am in the middle of history, in the middle of generations, in the middle of Danish fishermen and American flyers. I'm standing in the middle of memory and expectation because I did what middle children do best—I made connections.

* * * * *

It began with a letter. An old letter addressed to my father from Denmark when I was nine months old. Delicate cursive writing. Photos enclosed along with a newspaper clipping.

The letter was forgotten, stuck in my father's POW journal which came into my possession after my mother died. Dad's journal was tucked in a closet for two years until one snowy day in March 2017. On the anniversary of Dad's death, I flipped through drawings of airplanes and lists of books he read as a POW. There were pages of cartoons, poems and sayings, and even some old German newspapers, but Dad's personal story was missing.

As I closed the book, I noticed a fragile envelope tucked under the back cover. I tugged and four photos fell out—photos from 1943. My heart jumped when I saw my father in torn clothing, leaning on a boat rail, strong waves pounding in the background. These were photos from the rescue. *How did my father get these pictures?* I wondered.

Along with the photos was an aged newspaper clipping with my father's name in the headline and a handwritten letter from Denmark posted August 3, 1949. Since I couldn't read Danish, I stretched my hand across computer keys and across the ocean. I posted everything on my Facebook page convinced that someone would know someone who could help. In two days, I had a translation of the letter:

> *I remember you very well. Also your three friends I remember well…I hope you remember me and ask you to write to me and tell me how you have been doing in the past five years. Also, please, I would like information about your three friends. I will end with the warmest greetings to you and your family.*

The letter was signed, Svend Lundager Pedersen, Fishing Skipper. The skipper's care and memory overwhelmed me. He wondered (and so did I) about the other rescued crew members. Did they survive the war? Determined to connect with the families of the Danish fishermen and the surviving crew, I turned again to social media.

Michael Faley, archivist for the 100th Bomb Group Foundation, linked me to Jeanne Carey, daughter of Pilot Carey, texting, "Now you have another sister."

"We're sisters, indeed," I wrote back. "Our fathers survived together because a fishing crew found them in that unforgiving North Sea."

More sisters came when I located the daughters of the wounded gunners. I found Roberta in California and Judy in Oregon. Like Jeanne, they encouraged my search, passing along photos and facts to their siblings, children, and grandchildren.

Details about the rescue emerged from Denmark. I learned that Dad's quick thinking made a gesture that rippled for seventy-four years. Before he was taken as a POW, he gave his name and address to a woman at the pier who kept the story alive by writing for the underground press in Denmark—an occupied country in

1943. Six years after the rescue, her secret account was published and sent inside the skipper's letter.

Mathilde, a new intern at the same Danish newspaper, convinced her editor to feature our search. "I know I have to write the story and find the people, and I firmly believe it is possible," Mathilde emailed. "I want to spread the word. What I need from you: What would you say to the families if you find them?"

When Mathilde's two-page story was printed in April, Kirsten, daughter of Skipper Svend, was volunteering at the local hospital. Her phone (and mine) rang all day with good wishes as the news traveled. Facebook translated her joyous words. "When my nephew brought me the paper, I immediately recognized my father in the photos from the rescue. I never knew about his courageous decision to go after the Americans," Kirsten wrote. "I am bubbling with happiness."

I didn't leave my computer all day when Mathilde sent her story. I thanked Kirsten's family and gave details about our lives. "Dad married his sweetheart, Jane, after he returned from the war. Pilot Carey had ten children. The injured gunners survived…" Conversations rocked with emotion. More connections brought wonderful surprises.

Unlike Kirsten (the skipper's daughter), Jesper, the son of the photographer-fisherman, had known all along about the rescue. "As a kid, I listened to my father with tall eyes and ears when he told me this dramatic story. Now to find you, the daughter, makes a fantastic historic adventure." Jesper's next email gave me chills. "On the night of the rescue, your father gave his two silk maps to my father as a thank you."

Wow. I knew what Jesper meant. Thin silk maps of France and Germany printed on both sides were part of the escape/evasion kit to aid men if they parachuted from the air. Since silk wouldn't crinkle and announce a hidden airman, they were called silent maps. Nothing, however, prepared me for Jesper's next email. "Those maps are still in my possession. I would love to give you one—my pleasure." Jesper's package arrived in June.

The postal carrier had no idea his delivery had already survived a B-17 crash landing in the North Sea. He extended his arm and handed me the priceless gift—the silk map that once belonged to my father. As the mail truck pulled away, I opened the tiny box and read Jesper's note. "Hereby the legendary and beautiful map. I'm so glad to convey it to you. It has completed its last overseas travels."

Maybe it was just the sun on the front porch, but I felt my father's warmth as the silk rested in my shaky hands. I turned it over and over searching both sides. My pinky traced waves where Dad's plane had crashed. Breathing deeply I lifted the silent map to my face, careful to avoid the tears. But it *wasn't* silent at all. I heard the North Sea and voices from a summer evening in 1943.

An idea began to form in my mind. *What if the children of the fishermen and the children of the rescued flyers could meet?* By October, my wish came true. The 100th Bomb Group (my father's group) invited us to join them in Washington D.C. as honored guests. We would have a reunion *within* a reunion.

On the morning of the trip, I drove to a meditation garden to quiet my nerves. I walked along the labyrinthine path with a blue padded envelope resting near my heart. It held the original letter from the skipper, the news clipping, and the 1943 photos taken on the boat. As I reached the center of the labyrinth, I bent down and placed everything on the warm stone. After a moment of silent prayer for all our fathers, I picked up the blue envelope, wiped my tears, and turned toward the future. The anticipation of finally meeting face-to-face with all the connected families made me smile. I couldn't wait to board the plane.

Children and grandchildren of the flyers and fishermen came from all over the U.S. and from the east and west coasts of Denmark. As I walked into the dining room in my tri-colored dress, Mathilde, the Danish journalist, was the first to greet me. "And suddenly the world is just a small place where people meet." She quickly brought me to the center and picked up her camera.

When the handshakes and hugs slowed down, I placed the padded blue envelope in Kirsten's hand. It never felt so good to give something away. Kirsten shook as she opened her father's letter and saw his handwriting. "My father died when I was just fourteen," she said as she gave more hugs. "I never knew what he did—finding your fathers—but I am so proud. I'm filled with joy to meet everyone. I can't believe I'm here."

We had three days. Three days to remember and celebrate a time of courage and kindness during the inhumanity of war. And three days was enough time to become a family. Fifteen Americans, representing the ninety-eight descendants of the rescued flyers, and ten Danes, honoring the fishermen, became sisters and brothers for life.

On the last evening, at the formal banquet, I addressed the crowd of 350 participants from the 100th Bombardment Group reunion. American flags, which had flown over the U.S. Capitol, and engraved plaques, were handed to Kirsten and Jesper, who received the honors on behalf of their fathers. Each plaque said: "A person stands tallest when they bend to help another.

Our families exist due to your father's kindness. With eternal gratitude from the families of Richard Carey, William Styles, Robert Lepper, Maynard Parsons."

Stepping back from the microphone, I noticed again the three colors in my reunion dress. They are my reminders. Blue—for the ocean where this journey began. Black—not for grief, but for the strength of our fathers. And a bright white band—light to guide our new family.

As flags were raised, cameras flashed, tears wiped, there was a palpable sense of coming full circle—the familiarity of being a middle child. A middle child in history. A middle child making connections.

LEFT PHOTO: *St. Joseph's Cemetery, Troy, NY—Danish and American flags on the grave of Captain William J. Styles*

RIGHT PHOTO: *Linda Styles Berkery (left) and Kirsten Gaulshoj (right) daughter of Fishing Skipper Svend Lundager Pedersen, at the reunion of the 100th Bomb Group—October, 2017*

Dear Reader,

When I told a friend that I was taking a memoir-writing class, she replied, "Your life just isn't that interesting." And that might be true. I have led a very ordinary life. It was only when I began to reflect on my graced history through this collection of essays, that I recognized so many blessings and lessons.

It's important at various points in our lives to curl inward and reflect. My journey slowed for renewal near age seventy. That pause led me to dresses. Your memories might not come from dresses, but I encourage you, dear reader, to highlight and treasure your own blessings and lessons. We all have stories that are precious. Share them.

Linda

ACKNOWLEDGMENTS

When **Cara Benson** read *Brown Plaid in August*, the first "dress" story, she saw an entire collection ready to emerge. **Michael Welch** offered wonderful encouragement. **Robyn Ringler,** owner of **East Line Literary Arts,** brought the manuscript together through her dedication as an extraordinary creative writing teacher and editor. **Robyn** makes me a better writer and I am most grateful. This collection is the fruit of her guidance to find the deeper story.

Thank you to **Kathy Sowder, Rose Weaver, Eileen Anderson,** and **LucyAnna Rolfe** who read early drafts, and to **Lynn Ryan** who generously supported this work by her loving friendship. I am grateful to **Diane Cameron, Dr. Marian Condon, Nancy Putnam, Crystal Megaridis, Fran Rossi Szpylczyn, Cindy LaFavre Yorks,** and **Marilyn Walton** who wrote endorsements. I am honored by their beautiful words. Special thanks to **Alisa Anufrieva** for the dress photos and to **Meradith Kill** from **The Troy Book Makers.**

My sisters, **Janice Styles-Hall** and **Carol Hirata**, as well as my *new* sisters, **Jeanne Carey, Kirsten Gaulshoj, Roberta Greco, Judy Moore, Mathilde Jespersen,** and my *new* brother, **Jesper Skouenborg,** were in my thoughts as I wrote. To my children, **Leanne Goldberg, Jack, Tom, and Mary Berkery** and their spouses, **Jay Goldberg, Diana Berkery, Jillian Borden, and Matt Waskovics**, thank you for your loving support.

I am most grateful to my husband, **Jack Berkery**, who has hooked and zipped so many dresses in our fifty married years. Thank you, **Jack,** for your computer gifts, artistic talents, and your continued love. My eternal gratitude to Mom and Dad, **Jane and Bill Styles,** of blessed memory, who gave me my first life lessons.

Part of the proceeds from this book will be donated to Unity House and The Dress Project

UNITY HOUSE - TROY, NY
Making Life Better in New York's Capital Region

Unity House's Thrift Store, **ReStyle**, is located at 2431 Sixth Avenue in Troy, NY. **ReStyle** offers new and used clothing at affordable prices. The store offers clothes, shoes, and accessories by acting as a "broker" among people who have items to donate and people who have a need for those items.

Contact Unity House at unityhouseny.org
Follow Unity House on Facebook

THE DRESS PROJECT - ATLANTA, GA
Improve the World. Women Connected. Girls Educated.

The Dress Project collects like-new bridal and formal dresses and resells them to provide educational opportunities for young girls in Africa. Visit our dress diary to see photos and memories of dresses and how you can help. **The Dress Project** also accepts monetary gifts toward scholarships. Visit ***thedressproject.org/donate*** for more information.

Website: thedressproject.org
Follow The Dress Project on Facebook and/or Instagram.

Photo by Alisa Anufrieva